FOR LACK
OF A
SILVER SPOON

SEA·HILL
PRESS

Ordering Information: Special rates are available on quantity purchases by corporations, associations, and others. For details, please direct inquiries to orders@seahillpress.com.

Sea Hill Press Inc.
P. O. Box 60301
Santa Barbara, California 93160
orders@seahillpress.com
www.seahillpress.com

ISBN 978-1-937720-32-2

Printed in the United States of America

FOR LACK OF A SILVER SPOON

Christian Poems

by

Leonard Wood Sr.

SEA·HILL
PRESS

Santa Barbara

For the Lord heareth the poor,
and despiseth not his prisoners.

Psalm 69:33

Contents

The Spirit of the Lord God is upon me;
because the Lord hath anointed me
to preach good tidings unto the meek;
he hath sent me to bind up the brokenhearted,
to proclaim liberty to the captives,
and the opening of the prison to them that are bound.

Isaiah 61:1

From the Publisher

I received a package from Leonard Wood Sr. in spring 2014. Enclosed was a manuscript of his Bible-based poetry with a request that we consider publishing his work. He explained that he was in prison and during his time of incarceration had written the poems that are now housed within this book.

Due to our distance and other factors, we have only ever communicated through letters in which Leonard has explained his circumstances. It may be easy for any of us to pass judgment as to the reasons for his incarceration, however, the reader will most benefit not by focusing on these circumstances but from Leonard's willingness to adapt to them with his faith deeply rooted in his love for Jesus Christ. His deepest desire for this work is that it encourages others who are facing life's trials to reach out in faith to receive God's everlasting love.

Leonard Wood Sr. clearly is a man of deep faith. His poems present the living testimony of a man currently in a limited situation who has invited Jesus Christ to mold his life. This has allowed him peace in his heart and love in his soul. Regardless of his circumstances, his poems offer testimony of his love of Christ and encouragement for any who will hear.

Greg Sharp
Publisher

The just man walketh in his integrity:
his children are blessed after him.

Proverbs 20:7

A Man of Integrity

Life for me was never easy. When I was born, they forgot to put the silver spoon in my mouth. I had no father's love, only abuse and drunkenness. Raised by a single parent, my mother, who only had a third-grade education, my brothers and I grew up on food stamps and welfare. We wore striped pants and checkered shirts to school. We faced so much adversity. My mother always stressed: Be a man of integrity, a man of trust, honest, caring for others, and most of all be truthful, be a kind man, and love one another.

I will never forget those words she said to me nor the times she kept pressing me to better myself to valiantly overcome all obstacles in my way. My mother was proud of me. I graduated from high school in 1974, bought my first car, a candy-apple red 1970 Chevelle Malibu, worked in a factory called Rogate Industries, chrome plated parts for General Motors Corporation, married my high school sweetheart, and moved to Mobile, Alabama, where our two children were born, a daughter and a son.

We were happy until my wife deserted the family and left me with two children to raise. Being a young man in my early twenties, I was facing a lot of responsibilities myself, raising two children on my own; it never was easy. No one said it would be. I never gave up. Lost a few jobs along the way because I could never find a reliable babysitter. Learned how to be a good cook, a mother/father/housekeeper in one. Had a few doors slammed in my face by women who didn't want the added responsibility of helping me raise two children.

After six years raising two children by myself, the Lord blessed me with another wife. She accepted the two children as her own. Two years later we were blessed with another addition to the family, another daughter. Everything was going good. Bought a home, a three-bedroom ranch house in the country with an acre of land, owned a new car, a white 1992 Dodge Shadow, was part of a credit union, had a Visa and a MasterCharge, and was never unemployed or without a job since high school, attended church services regularly, a firm believer in Jesus Christ, who died for my sins and arose from the grave; and like everything else in life, it takes faith, good will. I remember my mother's words: Be a man of integrity, honest and caring for others.

In 1996, I lost my freedom and was wrongfully convicted. In open court I told the truth. I'm not guilty, and because of a severe injustice in our court system, the judge who had no judicial power, violated my Constitutional right to having a fair trial (withholding information that would have changed the outcome of the trial), tampered with the jury, and placed me in double jeopardy (he indicted me three times for the same offense), each time during all three trials I pled not guilty, and all because of a judge's personal vengeance.

I can honestly say that I'm suffering from a terrible miscarriage of justice. One I truly believe caused my mother's death in the month of January of the year 2000. You could say I was bitter; yes, I was. Or you could say I still carry emotional scars; yes, I do. But remembering what my mother taught me: Be a man of integrity, be honest, be kind, be true to yourself, and love one another regardless of what others may think, have faith, believe in the power of God to prevail. For He is the one and only true judge that I will stand before someday; nothing else will matter.

I will remain an man of integrity, a man of valor. With my faith in God, I am certain He will restore my life like Job in the Old Testament.

Leonard Wood Sr.

*For I know that my redeemer liveth, and that he shall
stand at the latter day upon the earth:*

*And though after my skin worms destroy this body,
yet in my flesh shall I see God.*

Job 19:25–26

For I am persuaded,
that neither death, nor life, nor angels,
nor principalities, nor powers,
nor things present, nor things to come,

Nor height, nor depth, nor any other creature,
shall be able to separate us from the love of God,
which is in Christ Jesus our Lord.

Romans 8:38–39

Jesus saith unto him,
I am the way, the truth, and the life:
no man cometh unto the Father, but by me.

John 14:6

With Jesus In the New Year

To Look forward to a Happy New Year,
You must Live for the Lord
Repent and Let Go of all your sins and fear
And believe within all your heart that Jesus
Died for you on the Cross and Arose from the grave
For He soon will be here.

He will not touch down on the Earth,
For He will come down from Heaven, in the sky appear,
Take His people from the grave and give them a new body
For in Heaven there is God's Love and no fear.

So you must think about your life today,
Where you're at, and what you have done.
For there may not be a tomorrow
When Jesus does come down, in the twinkling of an eye,
Are you ready to Lift Up your hand and say,
Here I am Lord with all my sins and sorrows
Thank you, Lord, for taking them all away.

Take me by the hand,
And Lead me into the Promise Land
For I have been faithful by reading Thy Word,
And with You, Jesus in Heaven, I will joyfully stand.

Dec. 2003

I Believe

I believe God created Heaven and Earth
set bright stars in the dark night sky
created all the planets, galaxies and the entire Universe
Not for scientists to dispute or to question why.

I Believe that from the dust of the ground, God formed Man
breathed air into his nostrils, and he became a living soul.
I truly Believe: Man was created in God's image and likeness
full of Love, Joy and Kindness
Not in a theory of Evolution, apes slowly developing into man.

I Believe Jesus is God's One and Only Begotten Son
and whosoever shall confess that Jesus is the Son of God
God dwelleth in Him, and He in God
for whosoever is born of God Believes
in the Father, the Word, Holy Spirit, these three are One.

I Believe without Faith it is impossible to please Him
for he that cometh to God must Believe
that He is God, a rewarder of them who diligently seek Him
with a pure heart, of a sound mind, and soul. This I Believe.

I Believe Jesus said: "Ye shall know the Truth
and the Truth shall make you Free."
"I am the Way, the Truth and the Life
No man cometh unto the Father but by Me."

I Believe Jesus said: The Spirit of the Lord is upon me
because He hath annointed me
to preach the Gospel to the poor, heal the broken-hearted,
preach deliverance and set the captives free
and restore the sight of the blind to see.

I also Believe Jesus said: "If any man will come after Me
let him deny himself, and take up his cross daily and follow me;
For whosoever will lose his life for my sake,
the same shall save it."

The People said: Save Thyself, come down from the Cross.
Jesus being found in the fashion of a man
humbled himself and became obedient unto death
Even the death of the Cross
I Believe without a shadow of a doubt in all my Heart
that Jesus did die for our sins on the Cross

I Believe that on the third day He rose from the grave
and is sitting on the right hand of His Father in Heaven
So you must Repent; give your life to the Lord
For a world of lost sinners, He came to Save.
This is what I Believe.

Nov. 22, 2013

*Whosoever will come after me, let him deny himself,
and take up his cross, and follow me.*

Mark 8:34

Two Thousand Nine

In the year two thousand nine
All human beings are living in a world of turmoil
Fighting over gas prices, and the rising cost of heating oil
The rich are getting richer, enjoying a game of golf on the back nine
While the poor are trying to scratch two nickels together
to make a dime

In the year of two thousand nine
There are people fighting, struggling, hungry
Standing in lines, out of work and angry
Needing a job so badly, so they can pay their bills on time

In the year of two thousand nine
We watched the stock markets plummet and plummet downward
Now the government is borrowing money from loan companies
all over town
While the politicians in Washington, D.C.
Are eating and enjoying steaks, and drinking wine
Figuring new ways to make us pay more taxes on property
That is paid for, and already yours and mine

In the year of two thousand nine
Violence is running very rampant, and at an all-time high
Street corners are filled with prostitutes, and drugs
Robberies and muggings are happening to whomever passes by
Mom and pop stores are getting hit by thugs
Shot to death, lying in a pile of blood just for a few dollars
Families mourning and grieving, and having a rough time

In the year of two thousand nine
Our factories like Hoover Vacuum Cleaners and General Electric
Have all moved to China, and are overseas
I remember when I was a lad, when jobs were plentiful
In the good old U.S.A.
Taking pride in products made in America
Government knows foreign trade ruined the U.S.A.
And I'm no longer proud to say, or live past
The year of two thousand nine

Aug. 30, 2009

Better is little with the fear of the Lord
than great treasure and trouble therewith.
Proverbs 15:16

Valentine's Day

Yesterday was Valentine's Day
I had no one out there that wanted to be
So very much in love with me
What a very empty, lonely feeling I had that day

I didn't receive a Valentine's card
Nor even words to say I love you
No sweet candy or red roses to later disregard
I just went through, the whole day alone and blue

I was just thinking of Valentine's Day
With cupids' harps and arrows flying above
And a love as pure, as a snow white dove
There was a person that I really needed to hold and say
I need you, my love please don't go away

For now years have passed us by
Our lives have went in so many directions
One for the better and one for the worst
And one wrongfully placed in the Department of Corrections
Now all I can do is sit back and wonder why

I want my appeals to go through
I so very much want to get out
To begin a new life with you
To take my time and try to find out
What true love is all about
And this time, not let it slip away

Feb. 15, 1998

You're Not Alone

Have you ever felt like you were all alone,
And it seemed like nobody was there?
Your heart and soul kept crying out,
"God help me in my times of anger and despair."
You were hurting inside, and you wanted it to be known

You started with an angry shout
And began to get mad and stomp your feet
God help me to begin to pout
My life is miserable, and I have no doubt
That it's over, and I no longer want to compete

The devil stole from me everything I had
Now I'm walking around in pain and misery
Very angry and upset and mad
Blaming God, why did you let this be
Why didn't you fight for me

Then I opened my Bible for which it had said
There is no temptation, taken unto you that is common to man
God is faithful; He will not suffer you, He said
To be tempted above ye are able, and can
With the temptation also make a way to escape
That ye may be able to bear it and withstand

Now that you know you are not alone
And there is someone there that really cares
Don't worry about anything let it be known
For God He will answer your prayers.

Oct. 1997

In the Spring

In the Spring I can Smell the fresh Air.
It Appears to me like Dead Things
Are ready and waiting to come back to Life.
Grass starts to turn green through the fields and yards Everywhere.

In the Spring I can Hear
Bluebirds and Robins with their beautiful melodies to Sing.
In the Spring I can Hear
The hard raindrops that fall on my Roof, *Ping, Ping.*
Thunder and Lightning is moving on, and the sky starts to Clear.

In the Spring I can Touch and Feel
A walleye fish nibbling at my Bait.
He hits and I struggle to bring him in, with my Rod and Reel.
He fights and tries to get away, I will not Hesitate
To throw him in my boat, and I will have him for an Evening Meal.

In the Spring I love to Taste
Hamburgers and Hot Dogs on a backyard Grill,
And wiping the Mustard and Ketchup off my Face.
Eating strawberry pie, and getting my Fill.
Drinking Pepsi, and leaving nothing to Waste.

In the Spring I can See
Beautiful flowers, Tulips and Red Roses,
Wasps, Hornets, and Honey Bees.
Families squirting each other with Water Hoses,
And I can See this happening to Me.

God gets all the Glory for bringing in the Spring,
Because He made all those wonderful Things.
Easter, for it will soon be Here.
It's time to come to all your Senses, and remember Jesus
Died on a Cross, and Arose from the Grave in the Spring.

Then shall we know, if we follow on to know the Lord:
his going forth is prepared as the morning;
and he shall come unto us as the rain,
as the latter and former rain unto the earth.

Hosea 6:3

Persuasion and Temptation

In the Garden of Eden there was a snake
Who persuaded Eve to eat from the forbidden tree
Eve saw that it was very pleasant for the eyes to see
And good for her and Adam to partake

The serpent said it was a tree to be desired
To eat, to make one knowledgeable of good and evil
Persuasion is what made them look, and to be inspired
Suddenly both of their eyes were open; they felt despised
Virtually naked and beguiled because of the devil

The Lord of the Philistines told Delilah to allure him, persuade him
Get Sampson to tell you where his great strength lieth
So we can bind him, cause him pain, torture him
Your reward is eleven hundred pieces of silver to inspire him

In our everyday lives we face so many problems and temptations
A lot of times we let out friends, and loved ones persuade us
To do things we don't normally do, to jeopardize our relations
We lie, cheat on our wives, drink, and do drugs, for our sensations
If we continue this life-style we surely will face hell and damnation

I was like that so many years ago, faced with temptation
Submitting to my pleasures and desires,
leaving nothing for my imagination
Now I'm being locked up in prison until my time is up, my duration
Praying for another chance, maybe a shot for freedom or probation

My judicial fight is over, I must leave it in God's hands
I've changed, no longer will I let the devil be in command
Neither will persuasion or temptation rule my life
And I'm so so sorry forgive me Lord for cheating on my wife

We all have experienced persuasion and temptation
We all have sinned and fall short of the glory of God
Thank you, Jesus, for dying on the cross for our redemption
For it is written again, thou shall not tempt the Lord thy God
Jesus is the only one that never gave into persuasion or temptation

June 8, 2012

For all have sinned,
and come short of the glory of God.

Romans 3:23

The World

The world was built by a wonderful man
Who had so much love in His heart
That He gave us land, water and air
That our life-styles would never part

Then came man
To corrupt the land
He built planes, ships and bombs
With the palms of His hands

The world was built by a wonderful man
Who had so much love in His heart
That He gave us land, water and air
That our life-styles would never part

Then came woman
Man fought over woman
Woman fought over man
For each other's dignity

The world was built by a wonderful man
Who had so much love in His heart
That He gave us land, water and air
That our life-styles would never part

Nov. 15, 1998

Brother Brother

Brother, brother, what is wrong with the world today
It's brother against brother
When we ought to love one another
And treat each other the same way

It's not about the color of your skin
Or whether you're black or white
Not hatred, or ill feelings you held within
It's not about who's wrong or right

We should just learn to get along
And not to fuss, and fight
And fill your hearts with a joyful song
To join hands together, with no evil smite

We need to be brothers
And look at people for what they are
Not where they come from
Whether from another country near or far

The world would be a wonderful place
If brothers could learn to love one another
And treat each other in the same way
All throughout the human race

Sept. 1997

Why Lord Why?

Oh Lord, Please Hear my Cry!
I have so many Questions to ask you Why?
Why? must I have to fight with the Devil
In a world that is so corrupt and full of Evil
Why Lord Why?

Be Alert your Adversary, your Enemy the Devil
is like a Roaring Lion, looking for those He can Devour
Especially the ones that are Corrupt, and Full of Evil
Resist, Stand Fast like so many in this World before You
who suffered, Pain, Afflictions, don't give the Devil any Power
After you have Suffered a while, God will make you Perfect,
strengthen you

Why? is life in this world a constant struggle until we Die
Why Lord Why? is our mind an ongoing Battle Field
Fighting over thoughts some good, and some Bad
Why? do we hold on to a yesterday we once Had
Why Lord Why?

Love not the world, nor the things that are in the World
if any man love the World
The Love of the Father is not in you
Be ye not conformed to this World
But be ye transformed, by the renewing of your Mind
may prove what is good, an acceptable perfect will of God in you
for a thousand years are but a yesterday in Time

Why? Lord do we need a suit of Armor and a Shield
Why? is life so rough at times, that we breakdown and Cry!
Why? do we want to give up, surrender, submit, yield
and look high up in the Clouds and Sky
Why Lord Why?

Put on the whole Armor of God, not tomorrow, Today
so you can stand against the wiles of the Devil
and shall not God avenge his own elect which Cry
Bear long with them night and day

Therefore submit yourself to "GOD"
Resist the Devil and he will Flee from you and your Evil
and then shall the Son of "GOD,"
Jesus will appear, so look High up into the Clouds and Sky
From Heaven Jesus will come with great Power and Glory
THAT IS WHY!

Mar. 26, 2013

And shall not God avenge his own elect,
which cry day and night unto him,
though he bear long with them?

I tell you that he will avenge them speedily.
Nevertheless when the Son of man cometh,
shall he find faith on the earth?

Luke 18:7–8

End of Times

Live everyday as if were going to be your last
So please my brother don't mention the past
Whether you may think you're right and everyone else is wrong
You must go on in life singing a glorious song

Just realize your life has spun way out of control
And there's nothing that you and I can do
In life you have to play the cards that are dealt to you
So step back and let the dice roll
When all you need to know is to let God in control

Brother will betray brother to death
Father shall be divided against the son, the son against the Father
Daughter against the Mother, the Mother against the daughter
Children will rebel against their parents
And shall cause them to be put in prison until their death

In the end times you will hear of wars and rumors of wars
State and National Governments will crumble and fall
Nation will rise against Nation for war
It will all boil down to the President to make the call
Then United States will unfortunately enter a global war

There will be massive earthquakes in different places on earth
People all around the world will be starving to death
Fighting over oil prices and the almighty dollar for what it's worth
Middle class people will be poor while rich enjoy their wealth

So live everyday as if it were going to be your last
So please my brother don't mention the past
Whether you may think you're right and everyone else is wrong
You must go on through life singing a glorious song

Apr. 10, 2011

A Light

Oh Lord I see
No light in front of me
Just pain and misery
Being away from my home and family

That my heart is filled with sorrow
Crying out in the night
Wondering what will happen tomorrow
Hoping my Lord will make everything all-right

I stumbled through the day
Feeling all alone and depressed
Expecting trouble to come my way
For the devil would give me no rest

I will fight for you
My Lord Jesus said
Live your life for me
And I will put Heavenly thoughts in your head

Oh Lord I can see
Through the darkness of the night a light
Shining in front of me
Arms just waiting to hold me tight
Leading
Me home to family

On a Summer's Day

On a very hot summer's day
In July sitting here sweating in my cell
I think of all the freedom I had yesterday
Wondering why have I been put in this man made hell

On some of those hot summer days
My family and I would take a vacation
In our car, traveling on a beautiful scenic highway
In a hurry to reach our destination

On a very hot summer's day
We often load our car, with a lot of cheer
As I took my family to find a cool lake to play
With the joy of hearing all the sounds of love and laughter near

I used to love those hot summer days
Flipping hamburgers and hot dogs on a grill
Having the family help out in their own ways
Screams of excitement haunt me still
On those hot summer days

I dream of them now as the days and months, turn into years
My hands held tight to my face streaming with tears
Wanting my freedom back to enjoy those hot summer days
Those hot summer days

July 2006

On a Windy Day

The Wind on a Windy Day
Whistles and Howls in a very Mysterious Way
The Wind can have the strength of a Hurricane
It can pick me up and then drag me Away

Also with the Wind on a Windy Day
I can take a Kite and with a real fast Run
Watch it Soar high up in the Air
Traveling around above Freely with little Care

Or I could Imagine I was an Eagle flying in the Sky
Gliding to and fro with the Wind so Free
Without these Prison Walls that are surrounding Me
With my Mind and my Spirit that I can Do
Especially on a Windy Day

And with the Wind on a Windy Day
I can also picture Myself lying under a shade Tree
After a long and Warm Summer Day
Taking a Nap and enjoying a Gentle Breeze
Then I awake and find Myself Dreaming
About my Freedom on a Windy Day

March 2004

A Form Of Godliness

According to God's divine power
He hath given us all things that pertain to life
And a form of that is to live a Godly life
He will send His son Jesus; no one will know what hour
That Jesus will come and take us into His power! God's divine power

You must be willing to give up all your foolishness
That includes pornography, adultery, fornication,
and excessive drinking
Marijuana, drugs, you don't need anything to cloud your thinking
It is essential that you turn away from the devil's darkness!
That my friend is another form of Godliness!!

I just want to clarify matters, on what I just talked about,
Getting high, and having premarital sex
Leaves so many of our young women fatherless
Lying, stealing, robbing, killing people is not what I'm talking about
That is not, I repeat that is not, a form of Godliness!!

When they crucified Jesus on the cross, He was harmless, and faultless
So please, my friend, ask Jesus our Savior to come into your heart
So He can take away all your foolishness, bitterness, sickness;
He was sinless
He died, arose from the grave, and is in Heaven with His Father
So if you slip and fall, we all do! So pray earnestly, believe
Ask for His forgiveness, that is a wonderful form of Godliness

July 30, 2011

Angry

God, sometimes I get so mad and Angry
When things I do turn out to be so Wrong
And someone's harsh words rub me the wrong Way
Please, Lord, help me to control my Anger
Stop it from coming out and causing harm to those around Me

Please, Lord, help me overcome my Anger
From wrongfully being locked up in Prison
For a crime I certainly know I did not Do
With so little regard of actual proof or Reason
Now, so many years have passed by, and Seasons
To a family I raised, I suddenly became a Stranger

Now I feel like a mad bull crashing through a Gate
With my nostrils snorting, face red and full of Anger
Charging at you, and not for a moment would I Hesitate
Putting my life or someone else's life in Danger

So if you're mad and angry with your Brother
Remember, the Lord said, "Let all bitterness, wrath and Anger
And evil speaking be put away from You
Be kind to one another, tender-hearted, forgiving to one Another
Even as God for Christ's sake hath forgiven You"

So, dearly beloved, avenge not Yourselves
But give no place unto wrath, for it is Written
Vengeance is mine, I will repay sayeth the Lord
So please do not try to resolve the problem Yourself
Jesus said: "Therefore if thine enemy hunger, feed Him;
if he thirst, give him Drink:
for in so doing thou shalt heap coals of fire on his Head."
And the Lord shall reward Thee

Feb. 15, 2011

Ready to Go

On this quiet Sunday morning,
I am sitting here all alone.
With a crushed and bleeding heart,
And it seems to me like everything I touch,
turns hard like a stone,
or dries up and falls apart.

My health has gone bad from a stroke,
Arthritis has set into my bones.
Muscles in my body went from strong to weak,
Bad circulation and numbness,
has set into my hands and feet.
Most of it was because I had a bad habit,
I used to smoke.

Pleasant words are seldom heard,
They are as sweet as a honeycomb.
Like listening to buzzing bumble bees,
And wings fluttering from a hummingbird.

Christian music brings peace to my soul,
Restores the joy to my broken heart.
My lungs are filled with a joyful sound,
Shouting I love you Jesus I love you Jesus
And now that is how I roll.

Memories, family and loved ones have all went astray,
Now there is nothing left, and I should die
In my sleep, rest assured, Jesus came for me.
I left the old plow in the field,
So my loved ones, please do not cry!
I am sorry I did not have time to say Good Bye!

Apr. 2009

Freedom

We fought the British
For our independence
In seventeen seventy six
For freedom that we all could cherish

Our nation was torn apart
In eighteen sixty five
North fought hard against the South
For freedom from slavery
That came deep from within the heart

I was born with my freedom
In the year of nineteen fifty five
Later a runaway flight to get married
Our daughter was born in nineteen seventy five

My son was born with his independence
In the bicentennial year of nineteen seventy six
I lost my freedom in nineteen ninety six
And was wrongfully sent to prison
Surrounded by a barb wire fence

There is no price on my freedom
That any man can pay
It can't be brought or sold at random
Or against my will given freely away

Jesus had paid my price for freedom
When he died upon the cross
On earth Satan took away, everything was a loss
In Heaven God gave me peace, joy, everlasting life
And love and my freedom

Oct. 1997

Forgive

For the Lord is good, and ready to forgive
He has plenty of mercy, for us one and all
And if you choose not to forgive
Into the depths of hell you will fall

For the Lord to forgive us of our trespasses
We must forgive others of their trespasses
No matter what someone has done to us
Or we will miss that ride, on that Heavenly bound bus

For God so loved the people on earth
That He gave us His one and only begotten Son
To Virgin Mary to give birth
Baby Jesus was born, so victory over sin can be won

So Lord look upon my affliction
And please, Lord, forgive me of my sins
In whom we have redemption through His blood
That we can overcome drugs, alcohol, tobacco and food addictions

When I say I can forgive
But what you have done to me
I will never forget
Is just another way of saying I cannot forgive
I still have so many many regrets

Remember Jesus said: "Love your enemies, bless them that curse you
Do good to them that hate you
Pray for them that despitefully use you"
Your reward is in Heaven because Jesus loves you

Is it easier to say thy sins be forgiven
Or to say arise and walk
Ye may know that the Son of Man
Hath the power on earth to forgive

Jan. 21, 2011

And when ye stand praying, forgive,
if ye have ought against any:
that your Father also which is in heaven
may forgive you your trespasses.

Mark 11:25

Faith

Faith have we not in our hearts
And minds to see
Faith enough to believe and say unto a mountain
Be thou removed and cast into the sea

Faith have we like Daniel
Praying three times a day thanking God from within
His soul to defile a King like Darius
Ordered then to be cast into a lions' den
Having faith in God to send an angel to help him

Faith have we like Shadrach, Meshach and Abednego
Not to bow down and worship a golden idol
And to be cast in the mist of a burning fiery inferno
Having faith in God to send an angel to help them

Those who turn their faith to Him
Whose lives are so wrecked by sin
When in their crushed condition repent
And have faith in Jesus, ye shall be born again

The Lord said if ye have faith
As a grain of mustard seed
Say unto the Sycamore Tree
Be thou plucked up by the root
And be planted into the sea
And with your faith in God He will see thee

Oct. 1997

Teach Me How To Pray

Oh Lord teach me how to pray
I'm lost in sin Lord and cannot find my way
Lord open up my eyes and ears this day
And teach me how to pray

Lord I need you so desperately in my life today
Please Lord teach me how to pray
For without You Lord in my life
There most certainly is no other way

Oh Lord teach me how to pray
I have been faithful by reading Thy Holy Word
And accepted Jesus Christ in my heart to stay
Jesus did die on a Cross, for my sins He did pay

Oh Lord teach me how to pray
Humbly I come into your house asking for forgiveness
Knelt down at the altar and began to pray
Then I gave my life to the Lord
Now I am lost in His loving kindness

Oh Lord teach me how to pray
And if I should slip and fall
With You, Lord Jesus, You will always show me the Way
To repent of my sins one and all
Oh Lord teach me how to pray
I want to be with You Lord come Judgment Day

Jan. 4, 2003

The Kind Man

The kind man is no man to Be
People in this world are cruel and deceitful to you and Me
Pushing and shoving, sometimes knocking you Down
Trying so hard to be First
With so little regard for human Life
And how it was meant to Be

Then I remembered what my Holy Bible Reads
If any man desire to be First
Then the same shall be last of All
And a servant to All

Yes the kind man is no man to Be
Being kind to others, may not Be
A way of life for You
But it just happens to be a way of life for Me

I choose to do a good Deed
Helping out when a lot of other people Won't
Feeding a hungry man who is in Need
Loving and caring, for Human Life
There's no word in my vocabulary, such as Don't

Yes the kind man is what I choose to Be
Saying excuse me pardon Me
And I'm sorry if I offended You
What words I say with my Mouth
Are so faithful and True
Jesus said he loves you, and is willing to die for You

Yea, they say the kind Man
Is no longer the man to Be
So in this equal world, opening a car Door
For a lady is really not for You
Myself, being considered a Kind Man
That was something instilled deep inside of Me
Since birth, so a kind man is what I choose to Be

Jesus, the kindest man of All
Walked upon the Earth, helping the lame to Walk
And the blind to See
Being loving and caring to you and Me
Just like "Jesus," the kind man is what I choose to Be

Dec. 2004

. . . and what doth the Lord require of thee,
but to do justly, and to love mercy,
and to walk humbly with they God?

Micah 6:8

God

I'm sitting here in the green green grass
With things going through my mind
Like a trumpet of brass
Things are empty like time

Not knowing what hour
That God will find
To take us in His power
And sweep us away

It may be near
So don't withhold your fear
Give your heart to God
And you will be His little dear

You will laugh and love
And walk streets of gold
Both my friend
For young and old

Jan. 1994

My heart is fixed, O God, my heart is fixed:
I will sing and give praise.
Psalms 57:7

Jesus

Oh Lord, You gave Your life for me
So I may yet live
Thank-you for everything
For You and the love You had to give

You were sent from a Heavenly place
From your Father Almighty God above
That You would free the world from sin
And You would give everyone everlasting life
All throughout the human race

All you ask us, is to believe
And to trust and obey
You traveled throughout the Holy Land
Teaching us God's words His way

Great miracles You performed on the Sabbath day
You came across a blind man
And then you spat on the ground, and made clay
And anointed his eyes
And told him to go to the pool and wash it away

They placed a crown of thorns upon Your head
And nailed Your hands and feet to a cross
A soldier pierced a spear in your side
Blood and water ran down the cross
And the people began to shout, hail the king is dead

Oh Jesus, You gave Your life for me
So I may yet live
Thank-you for everything
For You, and the love You had to give

Jan. 4, 2003

43

The Cross

All of Pilate's Counsel, Elders, and Chief Priests
who sought false evidence against Jesus;
and wanted to put him to Death on the Cross.
Many False Witnesses came before the Chief Priest
and accused Jesus of many things. Jesus said nothing.
Yet still they decided to put Jesus in prison for "something."

At the feast, Pilate was to release a prisoner. One man,
whomever the crowd desired to be crucified on the Cross,
one Barabas who committed murder, whose life was a loss,
or a man they called the "King of the Jews";
Jesus, the Son of Man.

The soldiers lead Jesus away into the hall,
clothed Him in purple, placed a crown of thorns upon His head,
cursed Him, mocked Him, smote Him, spit on Him.
Yet still he was willing to carry the Cross
for a world of lost sinners; one and all.

They placed Jesus on the Cross,
nailed His hands and feet on the Cross.
A soldier pierced a spear in His side.
Blood and water ran down the Cross.

Are you willing? And able to stand up to this day?
Pick up your own Cross and follow Jesus away?
into the Promised Land; Heaven is where we will stay
So Please! Give your life to the Lord before Judgment Day.

Jesus, I lay my sins down at the foot of the Cross
I come to repent, believing with all my heart
That You will forgive me of my sins one and all.
I knowing this: we are baptized into Jesus Christ's death.

I believe Jesus rose from death in the grave
And is in Heaven, sitting on the right hand of the Father
So all is left is the Cross.

Nov. 19, 2012

If we confess our sins,
he is faithful and just to forgive us our sins,
and to cleanse us from all unrighteousness.
1 John 1:9

Holy Spirit

I can feel a wonderful Spiritual presence in this place
Traveling back and forth at an exacerbating pace
He is a very warm and gentle sensation
That I feel running up and down my spine
Who has the power to change water into wine

He moves through my body so gentle and free
It is the Holy Spirit that is tingling inside of me
Sincerely I pray and ask Him to come into my heart
To free me from my anger and despair
Then He washed away my sins and gave me a fresh new start
Now I can feel His Spiritual presence everywhere

The Holy Spirit is now with me each and every day
And when the devil tries his best to attack
The Holy Spirit is there to knock him on his back
Yet still he will not give up trying to find another way
But just remember all you have to do is pray

Sweet Holy Spirit
Sweet Heavenly Dove
Sweet Holy Spirit
Fill my body up with God's wonderful love

May 2005

. . . for the Spirit searcheth all things,
yea, the deep things of God.
1 Corinthians 2:10

Thy Will Be Done

God did not promise sun without rain
Light without darkness or joy without pain
He only promised strength for the day
When darkness comes and we lose our way

For only through sorrow do we grow more aware
That is our refuge in times of despair
For when we are happy, and life is bright and fair
We often forget to kneel down in prayer

But God seems much closer, and needs much more
When trouble and sorrow stands outside the door
And then we seek shelter in His wondrous love
Praying He sends help from Heaven above

And that is the reason we know it is true
That bright shinny day, dark and sad ones too
Are all we can say: Thy will be done
And know that you are never ever alone
For God is your Father and you are one of His own

He staggered not at the promise of God through unbelief;
but was strong in faith, giving glory to God.
Romans 4:20

Let God In Control

We wake up and face so many trials, and tribulations
And problems in our lives, and obstacles in our way
Worrying how we are going to be able to make it through the day
Wondering if we can handle the situation

We all get mad, angry and distressed
Fight within ourselves because we don't have all the answers
Crying out to God, please help me through this mess
And saying, are You trying to put my faith to the test

So we wrestle back and forth in our minds
Seek and search, and may never find
Enough strength to drop down to our knees
And not to hold on to any anger and resentment please

We have to in our hearts let it go
And realize that God is in control
For if something happens we know it was meant to be
And we cannot change what God has in mind for you and me.

Feb. 2000

Turn us again, O Lord God of hosts,
cause thy face to shine;
and we shall be saved.

Psalm 80:19

God's Grace

Only God can move that mountain you face today
He's the only one strong enough to push it away
Yet you try hard to conquer the problem yourself and fall
So you must believe within your heart and soul, that's all
That only God's Love and Grace can save you today

Take time to stop and listen to God's quiet still voice
He'll whisper in your ear what He has commanded of you
Whether or not you listen and hear it's your choice
The carnal mind says it's your life, do what you want to do
But just remember when you slip and fall you had a choice
To listen to God's quiet still voice

Yes only God can move that mountain away
You have to learn to depend on God's Mercy and Grace,
Not yesterday nor tomorrow but today!
No one can save you from the human race
Only God's Mercy and Grace
His wonderful Grace can save you today!

Oct. 30, 2011

Trust in the Lord with all thine heart;
and lean not unto thine own understanding.

In all thy ways acknowledge him,
and he shall direct thy paths.

Proverbs 3:5–6

Joy

When you're on a roller coaster ride
It starts climbing a very steep hill
When it gets to the top, how do you feel
It comes racing down; your eyes are open wide
Joy and laughter are filling you up inside

When you find a very special woman
And you're very much in love
Cupids, with harps and arrows are flying above
Together you find, your lives share the same interest
Joy is in your heart when you both say, I do

Now you are married and happy too
Your wife gets pregnant, a beautiful little girl is born
Joy is bursting inside of you

You both get jobs and work very hard
One works nights, the other works days
Years go by and your love starts to fade away
A harlot tries to seduce you, and you let down your guard

Now you have committed a very bad sin
You should have thought it over from beginning to end
Then you got arrested, and sent to the pen
She files for a divorce, and you try to start your life over again
Joy is now gone, and there is no way to pretend

You never realize how much a sin can do
When half of your family leaves and deserts you
Now you are in a very bad place, feeling alone and blue
Then you can drop to your knees and repent
Asking God to come into your life, and forgive you

You go back and search in your mind
And try to figure out, where you went wrong
All the parties, and the one night stands, you will never find
Or will ever replace the joy where once did belong
But you must go on in life with harmony and unison

My brethren, count it all joy
When ye fall into diverse temptations
Knowing this, that the trying of your faith
Worketh patience, but let patience have her perfect
Work, that ye may be perfect
An entire, wanting nothing, nothing but Jesus to enjoy

Dec. 1997

But let patience have her perfect work,
that ye may be perfect and entire,
wanting nothing.

James 1:4

Heaven

Since I was a Boy, at the early age of seven
I wanted to live my life for the Lord and go to Heaven
I learned the difference by doing what is right
and the punishment for things I done wrong
my mind is a battlefield, everyday it's the devil I must fight

So every morning, I pray to my Father "God" in Heaven
to keep watch over me, protect me, guide me
far, far away from the wiles of the devil
and from thoughts that are corrupt, and full of evil
I must try my best, and do what is right
and think of "God's" loving kindness, for Heaven sake

Our thoughts, our opinions, even our conversations
should focus on "Jesus Christ" our Lord and Savior
we should act, conduct ourselves in Christian behavior
Repent, live a "Godly" life, die someday and go to Heaven
we cannot allow Satan, to jeopardize that relationship

He who blesseth himself in the Earth
shall bless himself in the "God" of truth
He that sweareth in the Earth
shall swear by the "God" of Truth
in Heaven former troubles are forgotten
nor do they come to mind

Heaven and Earth shall pass away
but my words shall not pass away
but of that day, and that hour, knoweth no man
no not the angels which are in Heaven
neither the Son, but only our Father in Heaven

"God" shall wipe away all tears, no more crying
no more sorrow, sickness, no suffering pain
no more violence, or afflictions, nor mental stress
and no more fear of death, or dying

I so much want to be, with my Father "God" in Heaven
leave this sinful Earth, it's no longer a place for me
I suffered enough, I want ever lasting life, peace, love, joy
and I want to walk by still waters, lie down in green pastures
with my Lord Jesus Christ in Heaven

Jan. 15, 2015

*That he who blesseth himself in the earth
shall bless himself in the God of truth;
and he that sweareth in the earth shall swear by the God of truth;
because the former troubles are forgotten,
and because they are hid from mine eyes.*

*For, behold, I create new heavens and a new earth:
and the former shall not be remembered, nor come into mind.*

Isaiah 65:16–17